LIFE
VICTORIOUS
CHRISTIAN

VOLUME ONE

APOSTLE PROFESSOR J.B. MAKANANISA

outskirts
press

Outskirts Press, Inc.
http://www.outskirtspress.com

ISBN: 978-1-4787-9171-3

Unless otherwise indicated, Scripture quotations are taken from the Holy Bible, Authorised New King James Version. Take note that the name satan and related names are not capitalized. We choose not to acknowledge him, even to the point of violating grammatical rules.

This book, all other books and materials of Apostle Professor J.B
Makananisa are available at:

Charis Missionary Church
Tembisa, Johannesburg
South Africa
+2711 893 5158, +2711 027 7962
www.charismissionarychurch.org
twitter @cmccharis
facebook - charis missionary church
You Tube – charis missionary church

FOREWORD

Christianity is not a religion but a lifestyle. Now we have to follow the commandments that have been given so that we become victorious.

Joshua was told by God himself; this book of the law (commandments) shall not depart from your mouth, meditate on it day and night and observe to do what is written so that you will be prosperous and have good success. **(Joshua 1:8)**

This book will help us to follow the commandments, to observe them and live the life that is required of us as Christians. By the death of Jesus Christ, we are made to be victorious when we believe.

The life of a victorious Christian will help you to maintain what is rightfully yours in Christ Jesus, and to understand and know all that was ordained to happen in the life of a Christian.

Let the anointing of the Lord open your eyes so that you can understand how to handle yourself.

Prophetess Doctor Eunice T. Makananisa

ABOUT THE BOOK

Life of a Victorious Christian is dedicated to every Christian who wants to live a victorious life. Every

Christian needs deliverance. This book is written to help Christians maintain their deliverance and blessings in Christ Jesus.

What is written in this book is mind-challenging, life- changing, and spiritually transforming truth from the Word of God. Your life will never be the same again after reading this book.

Literally thousands of people all over the world have been set free by the anointed word of Apostle, Professor J.B Makananisa through watching him on television; **Charis TV** and **Olive TV**. It is impossible for someone to hear the message, watch him on television as he ministers and not be encouraged, delivered, and transformed forever.

TABLE OF CONTENTS

CHAPTER **One**

AUTHORITY

Exodus 7:9

"When Pharaoh speaks to you, saying, 'Show a miracle for yourselves,' then you shall say to Aaron, 'Take your rod and cast it before Pharaoh, and let it become a serpent.'" (NKJV)

As believers, we ought to exercise the authority that God has given us. In the above verse, God sent Moses to Pharaoh to represent Him; as a leader, he was to take the Israelites out of Egypt. God was ready to show His authority because the mission that Moses was undertaking was very dangerous without authority. Many of us need to prove something to our enemies, but it must come from God, rather than just proving something from our own understanding. If we prove for ourselves, our proof becomes an entertainment; if it is from God, that proof becomes a miracle.

Pharaoh needed a proof, and he asked Moses where he came from and by whose authority he had come, since Moses did not have the right to enter Pharaoh's territory. God told Moses to tell Aaron to throw down his rod and it would turn into a snake. This is a miracle that magicians were able to do, but God knew that the serpent from Aaron's rod would be bigger than all the other serpents. The authority was assured.

John 1:12

But as many as received Him, to them He gave the right to become children of God, to those who believe in His name. *(NKJV)*

Children of God have the right to exercise authority in the name of Jesus. They have the right to say they are from God, the right to accept or deny, and God will approve. Authority is the approval that God gives you and accepts it also. God wants to give you approval concerning any decision you make; He will agree with you. Authority gives you the right to exercise power in everything. Whatever you bind here on earth, God also binds it in heaven. We need Christians who know that when they say anything on earth, God will approve it in Heaven because of the authority given unto them. As a child of God, you are the one to deny certain things in your life; you can exercise the power because of the authority given to you.

When a police officer comes to arrest you, he will come in uniform and he will arrest you, as he has authority over you. If now the officer comes to you without the uniform or without any proof of his profession, then you will overcome him no matter the age. Authority defines where you come from; if you fail, it tells us where you come from.

The problem is not that you do not have authority but that you are not aware, for if you were aware, you could not have allowed Satan to come close to you. In Matthew chapter 28, Jesus says that all power was given unto Him (Jesus) therefore, satan has no power over you.

Matthew 21:23-27

[23] Now when He came into the temple, the chief priests and the elders of the people confronted Him as He was teaching, and said, "By what authority are You doing these things? And who gave you this authority?"

[24] But Jesus answered and said to them, "I also will ask you one thing, which if you tell Me, I likewise will tell you by what authority I do these things: [25] The baptism of John — where was it from? from heaven or from men?"

And they reasoned among themselves, saying, "If we say, 'From heaven,' He will say to us, 'Why then did you not believe him?' [26] But if we say, 'From men,' we fear the multitude, for all count John as a prophet." [27] So they answered Jesus and said, "We do not know."

And He said to them, "Neither will I tell you by what authority I do these things. (NKJV)

Jesus was healing people, and they came and asked Him by whose authority He was doing all that which He was doing; healing needs authority. If you want to be successful, exercise the authority that has been given to you. Stop blaming God, for He has given you authority to move and change situations.

Authority is there to be questioned. People question you, and though you may be suffering, that does not mean you are weak. You are the one to prove that you are called by Jesus. Already, as a child of God, whatever you are facing is questioning your authority. The poverty you are facing is asking you to stand in your authority. Have authority to change your life.

Two things that increase authority:

- **Faithfulness**
- **Knowing whom you represent.**

We who have authority do not care if our situation is not going well, for we know the one we serve is neither weak nor a failure. Know who you are representing. Just know that all things are in order because He is there and aware. Listen to this: God said if you speak about authority, you will be filled with power; whatever you say, you will see results.

The moment you say a word, it comes to pass, for God wants to prove that you are coming from Him.

You cannot compete when you know the authority in you, and that you are the one to set approval. You can set the standard of the life you want to live.

LIFE OF A VICTORIOUS CHRISTIAN

Authority is waiting for you--just utter a statement. The devil does not want you to speak a word, for he knows that you are representing the one above. As a man of authority, I say to you that from this day onwards, your authority will be visible.

A man of authority destroys fear and is filled with faith. You will speak things and see them come to pass. To receive approval from above, you do not need to be a prophet; just be yourself, a child of God. If you say your enemies will fall down, God will approve it.

You do not need forty days of fasting to speak your authority. You have a key in your hands, authority; when you close, no one can open. God has been waiting for you to say something; do not waste any more time--say it.

When Jesus was resurrected, He proved His authority without any struggle. When Peter was failing with the disciples, Jesus said, "Hey, boys" (He called them boys, for they were failing). He told them to lower their nets to catch the fish. There were no fish, but when they heard His command they caught a lot of fish. Words of authority create what you are praying for. Although satan will disappoint you, say your words, and they will be performed. You can say whatever you can say, and it will come to pass.

BREAKING PRIDE

Psalm 10:4-5

[4] The wicked in his proud countenance does not seek *God;* God *is* in none of his thoughts.

[5] His ways are always prospering;

Your judgments *are* far above, out of his sight;

As for all his enemies, he sneers at them. (NKJV)

As a child of God who is born again, you need to break pride. You need to understand why we have to break pride. We are born with pride; the Bible states that we are born in sin, as our thoughts are without God.

Pride makes you to do things which are not approved by God; you become what you are not. When pride entered into the devil, he saw himself lifted up and above God Almighty, and he admired a wrong position.

Breaking pride must be our way of denying ourselves and coming back to be led by God. You need to ask God for direction in every path you take.

Proverbs 3:5-6

[5] Trust in the LORD with all your heart,

And lean not on your own understanding;

^{6} In all your ways acknowledge Him, And He shall direct* your paths. (NKJV)

When you break pride, you search for a right direction from God. I found out that a man's understanding is limited, and that is why the Bible says we need to have a mind of Christ to have direction--remove pride to receive direction. I found out that many people do things because others are doing it. We are busy copying other people because we are not asking God; instead, we end up directing ourselves, leaning on our own understanding and failing.

Job 33:15-17

In a dream, in a vision of the night, When deep sleep falls upon men, While slumbering on their beds,

Then He opens the ears of men, And seals their instruction.

In order to turn man from his deed, And conceal pride from man…. (NKJV)

When God speaks His word in our hearts, He will be breaking the pride within. Pride destroys what you have worked for in many years. You can still smile with pride while deep down inside your heart is dying, because pride makes you a hypocrite. God wants us to be ourselves when He speaks with us.

Everyone who lives on earth has an assignment.

When you have pride, you hide yourself and you become someone else; you become double-minded, and the Bible states that whoever is double-minded cannot receive anything from God. God wants you to become yourself; He does not want you to decorate yourself by the life of someone else. When God speaks, everything changes.

God wants us to be like Him--let us not lean on our own understanding. Do not interpret dreams by your own understanding; take the dream as it is, and ask God to direct you. Do not move if God does not want you to move, do not do what God tells you not to do. Pride will make you compare yourself with other people. Be yourself with your weaknesses, and do not pose to be big, because when God looks at you, you are small.

Proverbs 16:18

Pride goes before destruction,
And a haughty spirit before a fall. (NKJV)

Before you see yourself destroyed, pride is visible. What I know about God is that the more He blesses you, the more He humbles you, because you need Him more when you are blessed. You cannot be defined by what you are having--you are defined by God. You might be doing something, but you are not visible; allow God to define you.

Accept yourself, trust in God, and do not lean on your own understanding. God is on your side--He will never leave you. You need to break your pride and become yourself, and God will help you in your weaknesses. The problem of having pride is this: you will always see yourself as a person of a higher caliber than you actually are.

Obadiah 1:3

The pride of your heart has deceived you, You who dwell in the clefts of the rock, Whose habitation is high;

You who say in your heart, "Who will bring me down to the ground?" (NKJV)

You have to realize that pride deceives.

2 Kings 5:1

Now Naaman, commander of the army of the king of Syria, was a great and honorable man in the eyes of his master, because by him the LORD had given victory to Syria. He was also a mighty man of valor, but a leper. (NKJV)

Naaman almost missed his healing because of pride.

He was overcoming his oppositions outside, but at home he could not sleep because of leprosy.

Naaman's healing was not where he was expecting it to be.

He was to wash himself in the river Jordan, but he said he could not go there because of his position, as the river was dirty.

Many of us have been given advice, but because of pride, we never take heed of it. It was very tough for Naaman, because there were better rivers that he could have gone to, but he had to go to the river Jordan, which was very dirty, where he was going to get his healing. Naaman needed to pass through Jordan to enter Canaan, a land of milk and honey. God is on your side, and He will direct your steps.

CHAPTER **Three**

GOD PROMISES

Genesis 18:2-14

² So he lifted his eyes and looked, and behold, three men were standing by him; and when he saw them, he ran from the tent door to meet them, and bowed himself to the ground, ³ and said, "My Lord, if I have now found favor in Your sight, do not pass on by Your servant.

⁴ Please let a little water be brought, and wash your feet, and rest yourselves under the tree. ⁵ And I will bring a morsel of bread, that you may refresh your hearts. After that you may pass by, inasmuch as you have come to your servant. "They said, "Do as you have said."

⁶ So Abraham hurried into the tent to Sarah and said, "Quickly, make ready three measures of fine meal; knead it and make cakes." ⁷ And Abraham ran to the herd, took a tender and good calf, gave it to a young man, and he hastened to prepare it. ⁸ So he took butter and milk and the calf which he had prepared, and set it before them; and he stood by them under the tree as they ate.

Then they said to him, "Where is Sarah your wife?" So he said, "Here, in the tent."

And He said, "I will certainly return to you according to the time of life, and behold, Sarah your wife shall have a son."

(Sarah was listening in the tent door which was behind him.) ¹¹ Now Abraham and Sarah were old, well advanced in age; and Sarah had passed the age of childbearing.* [12] Therefore Sarah laughed within herself, saying, "After I have grown old, shall I have pleasure, my lord being old also?"

[13] And the LORD said to Abraham, "Why did Sarah laugh, saying, 'Shall I surely bear a child, since I am old?' [14] Is anything too hard for the LORD? At the appointed time I will return to you, according to the time of life, and Sarah shall have a son." (NKJV)

When God promises, He fulfills.

The scriptures are telling us about what actually happened to Abraham and Sarah; they were already old, meaning that they had tried many things until they had given up. These people had dreams, and the dreams were wasted because of time, but one day Abraham was moving around and he saw three people coming; when he saw them he was moved, for it was a time of his visitation. When visitation comes, what happens to you is that you will be moved to act. You must know that it is your time.

Abraham looked at the three men and invited them. He never wanted anything from them but just to bring them into the house. Whatever Abraham was doing, he did it very fast as he did not want them to pass for he believed that they were pregnant with what he and Sarah had been crying for, for many years.

After they sat down to eat, these people asked one question: "Where's Sarah?" They knew Sarah, as they understood her situation together with her husband. The promise came out that in the year to follow Sarah would be pregnant and give birth to a son. A promise is not different from a prophecy; this man spoke a word from God, and not from his own understanding.

When God promises, He fulfills His promise. When you look at Sarah, you find out that as she heard the men telling Abraham about her conceiving, she laughed a laugh of failure and unbelief. Many of you, when you hear the promise of God for your life, will laugh or become angry, for you know what you have been through to bring a solution to your situation.

Believe the promises of God and see them manifest in your life.

Romans 4:18-21

[18] who, contrary to hope, in hope believed, so that he became the father of many nations, according to what was spoken, "So shall your descendants be."* [19] And not being weak in faith, he did not consider his own body, already dead (since he was about a hundred years old), and the deadness of Sarah's womb. [20] He did not waver at the promise of God through unbelief, but was strengthened in faith, giving glory to God, [21] and being fully convinced that what He had promised He was also able to perform. (NKJV)

In this context, the meaning of promise is to be assured; another name for promise is agreement. Abraham and his wife, after they had agreed, were persuaded--that is, they were convinced. The situation was not looking good; the womb of Sarah was dead, but they were taken from what they believed and trusted what they heard.

You need to come out from what you know and come to what God is telling you. Abraham and Sarah were already tired and old, but they believed God; looking at themselves without hope, they trusted the hope they heard of God, doing what He had promised. They were told that when the time came, what they were suffering to get they were going to get; to them, this was a prophecy.

I want you to understand that they waited for a very long time, and they went to many places looking for help, but they failed. Sarah was not believing the Word of God as she was to be convinced; she understood her situation that it was not possible for her to become pregnant. They believed what they heard, and it came to pass in their lives.

I want to promise you, as long as you believe, no matter what your situation may be, you are getting your deliverance. The doctor can tell you that it is over, your sickness is incurable, it is not possible for you to have a child and that your time has passed. You are looking at yourself saying the time of pleasure is gone, the time of prosperity is gone, the time of healing is gone--but there is a promise from God; you have not seen anything yet!

I told you in the beginning, you need to agree, Abraham agreed, you agree with God by believing. When you believe, you are counted as a righteous person. The moment you say "yes," you stand where God is standing. You are in the right standing with God. It might be tough, but the agreement makes you one with God, and therefore, do not look at your situation but look at what God can do. It is your time to take what you have been waiting for; a miracle called Isaac is coming your way.

Hebrews 6:12-16

^{12} that you do not become sluggish, but imitate those who through faith and patience inherit the promises.

^{13} For when God made a promise to Abraham, because He could swear by no one greater, He swore by Himself, ^{14} saying, "Surely blessing I will bless you, and multiplying I will multiply you."*

^{15} And so, after he had patiently endured, he obtained the promise. ^{16} For men indeed swear by the greater, and an oath for confirmation is for them an end of all dispute. (NKJV)

When God promises, He is also looking at your patience, and that is what makes your miracle a genuine miracle. Your waiting is over, for God has remembered you. The more you wait, the more they talk, and the more they talk, the bigger your miracle.

Listen, when you read about the Prophet Elisha you will find that, as he was just passing, there was a rich woman whose money could not produce what she was in need of. The woman called Elisha as he was passing by her house; she perceived that this man was a Man of God and that she could not leave him.

The woman did something remarkable; she built an upstairs room where Elisha could sleep. She did not know that as Elisha was sleeping up there, anointing from above was coming down to the woman for a miracle. The anointing was coming and filling where the woman was sleeping--she had everything (was rich) **but** she did not have a child.

There is a "**BUT"** in your life, but do not worry about it.

The Bible says when she was at the door, the Man of God Elisha could not wait. I also cannot wait; you do not need to come closer to me, but your "**BUT"** shall be cancelled.

God is saying: "Tell my people that they must know their '**BUTS'** so that I will be able to minister in their lives." *A promise is fulfilled upon your hearing. You will say things that will manifest in your life.*

JESUS THE GOOD SHEPHERD

1 Peter 2:25

For you were like sheep going astray, but have now
Returned to the Shepherd and Overseer of your souls. (NKJV)

It is very important not to leave the Shepherd but to return to the Shepherd. Many things that happen in our lives can lead us away from Jesus the Good
Shepherd; without a shepherd, the sheep will go astray. Shepherds are there to guide and to lead the flock. Many of the problems that we face signify that God is speaking, saying that we are to return to the Good Shepherd. God is saying that He is a Good Shepherd; Jesus cannot be a Good Shepherd and then leave you.

Isaiah 66:11

That you may feed and be satisfied
With the consolation of her bosom,
That you may drink deeply and be delighted
With the abundance of her glory. (NKJV)

There are wrong shepherds who are looking at their own gain. A hireling cannot risk his life. If you want to know that you are under the protection of a Good Shepherd, believe in Jesus Christ of Nazareth, because He died for you; He took the pain which you were supposed to go through. Jesus is the Good Shepherd, but when you follow wrong shepherds, the moment you face problems they turn away from you because they are there for gain. There are wrong shepherds who leave you when you are down and out.

John 10:10-18

"The thief does not come except to steal, and to kill, and to destroy. I have come that they may have life, and that they may have it more abundantly.

"I am the good shepherd. The good shepherd gives His life for the sheep. [12] But a hireling, he who is not the shepherd, one who does not own the sheep, sees the wolf coming and leaves the sheep and flees; and the wolf catches the sheep and scatters them. [13] The hireling flees because he is a hireling and does not care about the sheep. [14] I am the good shepherd; and I know My sheep, and am known by My own.

[15] "As the Father knows Me, even so I know the Father; and I lay down My life for the sheep. [16] And other sheep I have which are not of this fold; them also I must bring, and they will hear My voice; and there will be one flock and one shepherd.

[17] "Therefore My Father loves Me, because I lay down My life that I may take it again. [18] No one takes it from Me, but I lay it down of Myself. I have power to lay it down, and I have power to take it again. This command I have received from My Father."(NKJV)

A Good Shepherd is there to fight the enemy of the sheep. We cannot fight our own battles for ourselves, for we are the sheep led by Jesus Christ our Shepherd. As long as you are a sheep, you do need to have a weapon to fight. There is danger of threatening your life, but Jesus has come to give you that life.

You need to know who you are in Christ Jesus by following Him, listening to whatever He says, and trusting Him all the way. In all that you are facing, let there be no worry; you might be going through a wrong place which is leading you to the right place. Your Good Shepherd is an enemy to your enemies.

There is no need to fight your enemies, for the Good Shepherd is there to fight for you.

Many Christians do make mistakes when they face tough times; they forget who they are following. Jesus is the same yesterday, today, and forever. It is not over where you are; you are not defeated, and if you believe, you are going to your destiny.

Verses 15-16 refers to the Gentiles. When Jesus Christ of Nazareth was living at that time, the Gentiles [us] were not living by the Gospel. You have been called to come and be led to where you belong.

Jesus is your Good Shepherd. Whatever you are facing, know that Jesus is aware of every situation you are in. Whatever you are facing, that must never make you to forget that in front of you there is a Good Shepherd taking you where God had called you to be. Jesus says, "**I have been commanded to lay down my life for you.**" What are you facing?

Jesus will fight until your sickness leaves you, until your enemies are done. He is saying, "**Rest, for I will fight for you.**" When heaven agrees, no one can say no; you are bound to be successful where He is taking you, and you will never fail. When the opposers are criticizing you, do not answer them; the more they oppress you, keep on following the Good Shepherd.

No matter what you face in life, know that Jesus is the Good Shepherd. Christians who follow Jesus will never be misled. Some people can define you the way they want; they focus on your failures not knowing the one who is in front of you. Start to develop a mind of following Jesus, and come out of the mind of men. Jesus sometimes allows your enemies to talk and does not want you to listen to them, but to hold on to Him.

"**You are bound to reach a level where people will no longer recognize you because Jesus will erase your history and your geography.**"

In verse 27-29 Jesus says:

²⁷ My sheep hear My voice, and I know them, and they follow Me. ²⁸ And I give them eternal life, and they shall never perish; neither shall anyone snatch them out of My hand. ²⁹ My Father, who has given them to Me, is greater than all; and no one is able to snatch them out of My Father's hand. (NKJV)

You are facing a lot of challenges because satan wants to snatch you out of the path of following Jesus.

Psalm 23:1, 4-5

The LORD is my shepherd; I shall not want.

⁴ Yea, though I walk through the valley of the shadow of death, I will fear no evil; For You are with me;

Your rod and Your staff, they comfort me.

⁵ You prepare a table before me in the presence of my enemies; You anoint my head with oil; My cup runs over. (NKJV)

Who is your Shepherd? Jesus said that He has come that your life may be in abundance. A Shepherd does not have fear, because He is there to protect His sheep. God wants to prepare a table before your enemies so that your enemies can be shocked by what He is bringing into your life.

The Good Shepherd knows that you have lack, but when you take Him, you will never lack; take Jesus as your Good Shepherd and you shall not want, for He will prepare for you. God has been preparing your table, for it is your time to rise up and take what belongs to you; stop complaining and stop struggling by yourself.

When somebody is preparing something for you, you wait; when God was preparing for you, your enemies were making a joke out of you, not knowing that a miracle was on the way. People who suffer too much in life are the ones who flourish too much, but God says, **"Enough is enough, rise up and take what belongs to you."**

1 Peter 5:4

⁴ and when the Chief Shepherd appears, you will receive the crown of glory that does not fade away. (NKJV)

A Chief Shepherd shall appear in your life that you may receive what belongs to you, and they will ask you what happened and you will tell them, "**Jesus Christ of Nazareth the Good Shepherd has happened.**" When the Chief Shepherd appears and manifests in your life, power will fall upon your life.

What you have been crying for will come down upon your life.

This is a voice I heard from God: "**It is not too late to move forward. Do not look at your age; rise, and move, and see where you are going, and I will bless you that I may be worshiped the way you want me to be worshiped.**" He is the Alpha and Omega, the First and the Last. You have been worrying for a long time; worry no more, for it is your time.

CHAPTER Five

OPPOSITION, PLAN OF GOD

Your territory and blessings will expand.

John 13:8-11; 13; 16-18

⁸ Peter said to Him, "You shall never wash my feet!"

Jesus answered him, "If I do not wash you, you have no part with Me."

⁹ Simon Peter said to Him, "Lord, not my feet only, but also my hands and my head!"

¹⁰ Jesus said to him, "He who is bathed needs only to wash his feet, but is completely clean; and you are clean, but not all of you." ¹¹ For He knew who would betray Him; therefore He said, "You are not all clean.¹³ You call Me Teacher and Lord, and you say well, for so I am.

¹⁶ Most assuredly, I say to you, a servant is not greater than his master; nor is he who is sent greater than he who sent him. ¹⁷ If you know these things, blessed are you if you do them."

Jesus Identifies His Betrayer

¹⁸ "I do not speak concerning all of you. I know whom I have chosen; but that the Scripture may be fulfilled, 'He who eats bread with Me* has lifted up his heel against Me.'" (NKJV)

Jesus was explaining to His disciples about the washing of feet, but they were failing to understand.

When He was about to wash Peter's feet, he (Peter) wanted Jesus to wash his hands and head as well, because washing his feet alone was not enough for him. Jesus said if He could not do this to him, then it meant that Peter was not with Him but against Him.

Jesus knew everybody, and He knew the one who was against Him. No one understood what He was doing. Jesus knew His betrayer Judas Iscariot, but He washed the feet of all His disciples, including the feet of Judas Iscariot. It is not easy to love everyone to the level of Jesus; He knew His opposition but kept it to Himself and never fought back. He knew it was the Plan of God. I want to speak about opposition, for it is the Plan of God for you. Jesus knew the people who were opposing him.

In verse **16** of John chapter **13,** Jesus was saying that though you know your opposers, do as He did. Do not allow the opposition to change the plan of God in your life or bring any obstruction to where you are going; do not concentrate on the opposition when you know where you are going. I have never read about Jesus concentrating on Judas; today when you are opposed, you need to stand up and begin to praise God.

Opposition is there, according to Jesus, to take you away from where you belong. If Jesus had told the disciples what Judas Iscariot was going to do to

Him, they could have killed Judas and the plan of

God, for Jesus was going to fail--only Jesus knew the plan. He knew that when He was betrayed, it was for Him to go to the Father to take His own position.

You are not aware that the opposition you are facing is good for you, so that you will be able to go where you belong.

There are two kinds of opposition:

- **External Opposition**
- **Internal Opposition**

Jesus was facing an internal opposition; Judas Iscariot was so close to Him, and he was also in charge of His finances. There are people around you who are internal opposers deployed by Satan to affect you negatively. Do not worry, for the one who opposes you will never be better than you. I began to understand that all opposers around us are conveying a message to us, saying: **"Where you are, it is not your place; you belong somewhere else!"**

The moment you face opposers, do not look at where you are, but look at where you are going. Do not be redirected by wrong people.

This is how internal and external opposition work:

- **External Opposition is there to destroy your image and your character so that people will speak against your Christianity.**
- **Internal Opposition is there so that your faith may be destroyed.**

Sometimes you trust people who later disappoint you, and they end up looking down on you. Many people today are killed by internal opposition since external opposers cannot kill you, as they do not know much about you. The internal opposer of your life will always keep track of your life--but do not be in despair, for no opposer can overtake and overcome you, no one!

Many people today have embraced wrong people in their lives who have in fact worked against their lives, causing them to dry up. Jesus knew Judas Iscariot as an oppose. Know your opposers, for if you do not, you will be ignorant. The work of opposers is that they want your life to remain stagnant; they block your progress, for they failed in their missions and have come to destroy yours, but fear not, as they will fall down and you will walk on top of them.

Do not compromise; know your Jesus to walk on top of your opposers. This is the right time to leave the opposers behind you. Opposers are there to make you to think that your destiny is impossible.

They (your opposers) pose to be seen and talk to be heard so that you can be discouraged. Do not compromise your stand.

The disciples never knew where Jesus was destined to go until Judas went out and He was then able to tell them about His betrayal. Judas never heard that. There are issues in your life that your opposers must never know.

When God lifts you up, you will meet your opposers going down. God is saying to me that many of you are in a wrong position and He has sent me to speak against your opposers; they will never know how you entered into your destiny.

I am not much worried--I also had opposers, and where are they now? You will search for them, but you will never find them. There is a Glory that changes the situation you are in; there is an anointing to change your situation, for you are bound to go where you belong. Do not worry about your opposers; no door will be closed in front of you. People around you will envy you. Do not waste time, go to where you belong, move and you will not die there--God will do a miracle. WHEN YOU SEE OPPOSITION, REJOICE.

CHAPTER Six

OVERCOMING SIN

1 John 3:5-6

⁵ And you know that He was manifested to take away our sins, and in Him there is no sin. ⁶ Whoever abides in Him does not sin. Whoever sins has neither seen Him nor known Him. (NKJV)

Sin is our enemy. We are all Christians, but categorized in different levels of sin; behind every sin there is a demon. The meaning of sin means: **satan in**—therefore, the moment you sin, you open the door for satan to come in. It is useless to come to church as long as you know your sins and are doing nothing about them.

A Christian has a conscience, and before you do something wrong, there is a feeling you ought to feel.

Every Christian has awareness, which is derived from consciousness. Think before you talk; live like a child of God. The sin you do tells us that you have not seen God, and you do not to know Him.

We all have our weaknesses and we need God to help us in the area where we are weak. We are not to dwell in our weakness, for it is the one that makes us stronger, drawing us nearer to God.

James 4:17

Therefore, to him who knows to do good and does not do it, to him it is sin. (NKJV)

Too much knowledge regarding the word of God is very dangerous. The more you come to church, the easier it is to go to hell, for if you do not do good, it is a sin. SIN IS OUR ENEMY. Our goal must be heaven. The reason why we are dying here (on earth) is because our eyes are focused here (on earth) rather than focusing on heaven, because many people have made their bellies to be their god. Sin will always make us lose the best things. You cannot open the doors of heaven if you cannot open them here.

Your reality of worship is when you hate sin, but if now you are worshiping with sin, you will be closed here and in heaven, meaning that your worship will be diluted by your sin. If your consciousness is dead and you are struggling with sin, find strategies to fight it or stay away from it.

Let us find where our conscience is not working; when your conscience is not working, you can hide your sins. It is useless to serve in the house of God when you continue to live in sin.

Romans 3:23

For all have sinned and fall short of the glory of God. (NKJV)

Christians have a standard that God has set for them; sin breaks that standard that God has given you, the standard of Life. You cannot judge a Christian, because God has His own standard for everyone. There is a standard that God has set, and whether you are facing tribulations or not you will always have peace. What we are supposed to be is determined by what we are doing. Never judge your level, for what is important is to hate sin.

Psalm 32:1

Blessed is he whose transgression is forgiven, whose sin is covered. (NKJV)

The reason why we are going down in our lives is not because God is not aware; it might be that you are not aware. You need to check your life, always. When you come to God, people around you remember your past sins, but God is there to cover them.

Do not judge yourself by the sins of yesterday, for through repentance, God will cover your sins. You need to know yourself, that you may not be reminded by satan of your past mistakes.

You are not blessed because of certain possessions in your life but by your righteous stand with God. You will be the one to cover your sin if you are not aware of your weaknesses; you make yourself appear righteous before people, whereas before God you are wicked.

This is the mistake we are facing; we go by groups talking useless things which are not biblical. It is only when you pray that satan and demons watch you. In this world, there are desires, so it is not easy to leave sin. You will be willing to stop sin if you know the principles in the Word of God. You can be like Lot, who did not want his children to be part of the wickedness of Sodom and Gomorrah.

Once sin conquers you, it is no longer you who live, but sin. Sin is very dangerous; please know your sins! The moment you confess and stop sinning, you become holy. If there is a sin you continually repeat and you are always confessing it, know that your conscience in that area is dead. It is very dangerous not to be aware of your sin. Do not condemn yourself; just come back to God.

Galatians 5:17-20

[17] For the flesh lusts against the Spirit, and the Spirit against the flesh; and these are contrary to one another, so that you do not do the things that you wish. [18] But if you are led by the Spirit, you are not under the law.

[19] Now the works of the flesh are evident, which are: adultery,* fornication, uncleanness, lewdness, [20] idolatry, sorcery, hatred, contentions, jealousies, outbursts of wrath, selfish ambitions, dissensions, heresies…. (NKJV)

The Bible is a mirror of our soul; you can take the Bible and check if you are living right. Then if not, you must pray to God and ask for forgiveness. Life is too short. Verse 17 of Galatians chapter 5 tells us that by living right you will be edifying your spirit; never try to protect yourself.

If you are a child of God, you must know that your soul and the Spirit of God upon your life are very important, so you need to be edified and be led by the Holy Spirit. The more you are in spirit, the more you cannot see the flesh. There are certain television programs that we need not to watch as Christians, for you will become what you are watching.

The Bible tells us that where your riches are, your heart is there, so you must watch where you are spending your time. Let us show that we are children of God by living in unity with one another. We need to know where we are failing, and we are not to justify ourselves; nor are we to protect ourselves.

Every Christian has a discerning spirit; therefore you are to know what is good and evil. You need to reach a level at which you hate sin. When the light of God is too much in you because of the Word of God, people around you will not do wrong, for the light will expose the wrong in them and reprimand them. This is not the time to hide people's sins, though they may be close to you, for we are the light of the world. Where do you belong?

Checking your heart will help you to recognize that there is sin in you, and if you judge yourself, no one will judge you. We need to be conscious in doing what is right all the time. A Christian can still be sick of any disease, but what is important is your response to the sickness--sometimes God can allow you to live longer so that you may repent.

Let us try to check our lives; when our conscience is weak, we make mistakes. Confessing one sin every time can destroy your conscience, you end up getting used to your sin. Heaven is our home; know your area of sin that you may be able to deal with it.

We need to learn that it is not money that makes us better but God, for money can make you to be stingy.

Romans 7:17

But now, it is no longer I who do it, but sin that dwells in me. (NKJV)

1 John 1:8-9

⁸ If we say that we have no sin, we deceive ourselves, and the truth is not in us. ⁹ If we confess our sins, He is faithful and just to forgive us our sins and to cleanse us from all unrighteousness. (NKJV)

When we say we have no sin, we are liars; we need to check our lives every day. We need to be aware of our sins so that God may forgive us. What works well in a Christian's prayer life is peace, and as a sinner there is no way you can have peace. You must confess your sins!

CHAPTER Seven

OVERCOMING YOUR GUARDS

1 Peter 5:8

Be sober; be vigilant; because your adversary the devil walks about like a roaring lion, seeking whom he may devour. (NKJV)

When God is with you, it is not over; you will realize that the devil is around there. I found that everybody is surrounded by guards. There are two different kinds of guards:

- One to protect from harm
- The other guard is there that you cannot escape.

The Bible tells us to be sober; beware, because though you have guards around you to protect you from harm, there are other guards that are causing pain that you may not escape, and the devil is the source of that. He guards and makes sure that you do not escape. Know that there is a devil around you. He is not far, and he wants to make sure, if he is guarding you, that he searches for an opportunity to enter you. You have been guarded, but you are escaping.

1 Corinthians 10:13

No temptation has overtaken you except such as is common to man; but God is faithful, who will not allow you to be tempted beyond what you are able, but with the temptation will also make the way of escape, that you may be able to bear it. (*NKJV*)

Guards are there either to protect you or to make you a prisoner. There are many people who are in prison who cannot go where they desire to go. You have been in prison because of poverty, lack, pain, worry--and you tried to escape, but there is no way.

Mark 3:27

No one can enter a strong man's house and plunder his goods, unless he first binds the strong man. And then he will plunder his house. (*NKJV*)

This is how you can escape! There is a strong man guarding your possessions, and if you want to take those possessions, the first thing you do is to bind the strong man. You cannot get what you want because of the strong man in your life. You need to be stronger than the strong man to get hold of your possessions; do not come to an agreement with the strong man.

God does not want you to compromise in your blessing but to enjoy it. Bind the strong man in front of you and take whatever is guarded by the strong man.

This is not the time to beg your enemies or your opposers. Be stronger than them, be stronger than your sufferings and tribulations. Do not beg satan; he is there to guard you so that you may not pass and get what belongs to you.

There are people watching to see your God--they are there to give you direction that you may not take your possessions. Remove the strong man to change their topic.

Acts 12:1-9

Now about that time Herod the king stretched out his hand to harass some from the church. ² Then he killed James the brother of John with the sword. ³ And because he saw that it pleased the Jews, he proceeded further to seize Peter also. Now it was during the Days of Unleavened Bread.

⁴ So when he had arrested him, he put him in prison, and delivered him to four squads' soldiers to keep him, intending to bring him before the people after Passover.

Peter Freed from Prison

⁵ Peter was therefore kept in prison, but constant* prayer was offered to God for him by the church. ⁶ And when Herod was about to bring him out, that night Peter was sleeping, bound with two chains between two soldiers; and the guards before the door were keeping the prison.

⁷ Now behold, an angel of the Lord stood by him, and a light shone in the prison; and he struck Peter on the side and raised him up, saying, "Arise quickly!" And his chains fell off his hands. ⁸ Then the angel said to him, "Gird yourself and tie on your sandals"; and so he did. And he said to him, "Put on your garment and follow me."

⁹ So he went out and followed him, and did not know that what was done by the angel was real, but thought he was seeing a vision. (NKJV)

The moment you stand up, your guards will be silenced. The chains that where holding your hands will fall. Do not care about your guards; leave your chains, for your problems are going to your guards. Those who are guarding you will be imprisoned.

They know the potential that you have, and that is why they are guarding you.

They have been checking you; they will go and check you again, and they will find that you are no longer there. Do not judge yourself by your present situation, but believe that you are passing. The guards who were guarding Peter thought that the following morning he could be a dead man, but they did not know that there was a visitation from above.

If you read how Jesus rose from the dead, you will find the Pharisees and Scribes going to Pilate and telling him that Jesus would deceive the disciples, as they would come and steal Him; and they suggested to Pilate that they must assign guards to guard His tomb.

They put a guard and a statement which wrote: "**With Jesus it is over**" and they put a seal.

Something happened. Angels descended from above, the guards fell like dead people, the stone rolled away, and Jesus came out and went somewhere. Someone is checking you, but they will never know how you rose. They will try to copy you, but they will never be able to imitate you. Angels will take you out of the grave you are currently in.

They call you a deceiver because you are believing the promises of God, as His promises are "**Yes**" and "**Amen.**" The promises are about to manifest in reality because an angel from above will descend and you will come out from the grave and leave your enemies falling.

There was a seal which said you will not come out, but resurrection power has come. Do not look at what satan has done or is doing to you; your guards shall fall. Your address is from above, but your enemies' address is beneath. You live in the supernatural--nothing can chain you, and nothing can block you. Wherever you want to go, you will go. You cannot be blocked, you cannot be witched, and nothing can stop you, because Jesus is on your side.

CHAPTER **Eight**

PERFECTION

Proverbs 11:20

Those who are of a perverse heart are an abomination to the Lord, but the blameless in their ways are His delight. (NKJV)

God wants us to be perfect. The heart scans everything that can be detached only by God Himself, but God is ready for His people and enjoys people who are perfect. God is still searching for perfection in His people.

Matt 5:38-48

38 "You have heard that it was said, 'An eye for an eye and a tooth for a tooth.'* 39 But I tell you not to resist an evil person. But whoever slaps you on your right cheek, turn the other to him also. 40 If anyone wants to sue you and take away your tunic, let him have your cloak also. 41 And whoever compels you to go one mile, go with him two. 42 Give to him who asks you, and from him who wants to borrow from you do not turn away.

Love Your Enemies

43 "You have heard that it was said, 'You shall love your neighbor* and hate your enemy.' 44 But I say to you, love your enemies, bless those who curse you, do good to those who hate you, and pray for

those who spitefully use you and persecute you,* [45] that you may be sons of your Father in heaven; for He makes His sun rise on the evil and on the good, and sends rain on the just and on the unjust.

[46] For if you love those who love you, what reward have you? Do not even the tax collectors do the same? [47] And if you greet your brethren* only, what do you do more than others? Do not even the tax collectors* do so? [48] Therefore you shall be perfect, just as your Father in heaven is perfect. (*NKJV*)

The above scriptures show that we must resemble our Father by perfection. In this chapter, God is talking about our response towards other people. He wants us to be like Him, and if you can be like God, then it is easy to be blessed.

How do you relate to other people? God wants you to relate to your friend the very same way you will relate to an enemy, but if you relate to your enemy in a bad way, you are saying that you are not of God.

Your reward comes from your response towards those who hate you. It is what you do to those who are not of the same mind as you that matters most. A blessing is there when you bless those who hate you--this is a principle of life, of being perfect. Are you perfect?

Our response towards other people affects our prayers. God can send rain to the just and unjust. Whoever might be against you, know that person is holding your blessing. Your blessings can also be affected by the people you love so much.

You spend much of your love towards them, and on the other side causing stagnation in your life. It is not easy to be perfect, since everyone on earth wants to justify themselves.

The problem we have is that we always want to prove a point to our enemies. When you bless your enemy, you curse that enemy. God will bless you; so as the Bible says, "**Be perfect as your Father is perfect.**"

Colossians 3:14

But above all these things put on love, which is the bond of perfection. (NKJV)

When your response to your enemy is right, know that you are taking your blessings. Love is a bond of perfection--love your enemies! Never talk bad about someone, as that person might be holding your blessings. We usually justify ourselves by the weaknesses of others.

In everything you do, God puts a mark, and people also mark. We need Christians who live for God's marking rather than the marking of men. We use many of our friends' weaknesses to make ourselves better; this is not perfection but justification. God cannot bring blessings to people who always justify themselves.

Psalm 18:32

It is God who arms me with strength, and makes my way perfect. (NKJV)

Psalm 37:18

The Lord knows the days of the upright, and their inheritance shall be forever. (NKJV)

As a child of God, the strength of the Lord makes you perfect. When you rely on your own strength, ability, and understanding, you fail and feel unworthy to live.

Whoever provokes you makes your destiny difficult. When we listen to people who speak negative things, it brings obstruction to where we are going. God gives us strength to do what He wants us to do; continue doing good, though it maybe be tough.

The strength of the Lord will make you have power to move where you belong. You need to know where you are going, stop complaining, and deal with yourself. Do not listen to what people are saying about you, for how you respond to what they are saying about you matters--do not come out of your perfection. When you are perfect, your miracle is sure. Deal with yourself.

Psalm 119:1

Blessed are the undefiled in the way, who walk in the law of the Lord! (NKJV)

1 Corinthians 13:10

But when that which is perfect has come, then that which is in part will be done away. (NKJV)

Blessed is the one who walks in the ways of the Lord. He who is perfect when He comes, the imperfect will run away. When God makes you perfect, you reach a place where everywhere you go, you are the one to take control.

Let us not try to prove that we are perfect, there are blessings and testimonies which look like they are perfect, but you will come up with a bigger testimony as you hold on to perfection with God.

Do judge yourself and look at your present situation. The Bible says that the creation has been waiting for the sons and daughters of God to manifest. I see you coming and taking your stand and reaching your goal.

When you are perfect, you will produce all that is perfect: a perfect job, a perfect marriage, a perfect home, and a perfect business. When people look at you, they must see that you are a child of God. Perfection is your portion; it is your life and it must be your way of life.

You cannot compete with the children of God when it comes to perfection.

Luke 6:40

A disciple is not above his teacher, but everyone who is perfectly trained will be like his teacher. (NKJV)

A fake thing comes before reality; when you are moving, the sun is in front of you and the shadow will be behind you, but when the sun is behind you hitting you at the back to move you forward, the shadow will be in front of you. Do not be afraid of the shadow, for it is telling you that you are going somewhere.

All the imperfection in your life is there to tell you that you are going somewhere. Many have been competing with you with their shadows behind them; do not look at them. The heat at the back shows that your destiny is closer. Just move forward without looking back. Carry on doing what God says--love your Jesus and worship Him.

You may look like you are going down, but you need to know that Jesus is there to lift you and to raise you.

CHAPTER Nine

PERMANENT TEMPTATION

There are different types of temptations that we face as Christians. In this chapter we are going to talk about only two kinds of temptation: permanent and temporary temptation.

A temporary temptation is there so that when you pray, it will be approved, but no one will know it was there; when you are blessed, you even forget that you were once poor. The temptation I want to speak about is a permanent temptation, which leaves a scar in your life--you cannot change it, but you will have to go through it.

One can say that good people do not have to face bad things, but a permanent temptation is there to prove your enemies wrong. Permanent temptation is there, and will leave a scar that your enemies will see, but it will never stop you from reaching your destiny. Unless you prove your enemies wrong, you will never prove to them that God is alive. If you want to change your enemy's topic, overcome your permanent temptation.

Many times when you are tempted, you will face tough situations, but you must not be desperate. Jesus faced a temporary temptation when He was led by the Holy Spirit into the wilderness but was not desperate. It was only when Jesus was hungry that satan came to tempt Him. satan will never come if you are still able to kick your kicks; he will come when you have kicked your last kicks. Many of you have tried many things to come out of your temptations.

When Job faced a permanent temptation, he lost all his belongings, including his children. When he got a report that everything was gone, he never sinned against God, though he was afflicted. You can prove your permanent temptation wrong by not sinning.

The moment you try to protect your temptation, you sin, and when you try to establish your stand you also sin. You have a child out of wedlock, you are not married--this is a permanent temptation, as you cannot take the child back.

We need Christians who have scars but do not dwell in them. Many have been affected by their past stopping them from their dreams; I want Christians who have the right mind to overcome their permanent temptations, and who do not care about their past because God is doing it.

On permanent temptation, there are those who assume they know you better because of your situation, but they do not really know you, for when you overcome they will know you. They might have said you are a failure, but I say to you, "You are not a failure." They said you are poor but I say, "You are blessed." Overcome your permanent temptation and prove your enemies wrong.

God called Jeremiah, but there was a scar in his life.

Jeremiah was still limited because of the geography of his past; Saul did the same by saying he was a child of the least tribe of Benjamin. You can be born from a family which is not known, but through you, your family will be known. They might see your scar, but the surname will not affect you.

A permanent temptation is there to render the whole generation useless. The moment you move around, your contemporaries define you by your family's weaknesses.

Your family might know your tribulations, but rejoice and see the end, for that is where you are going. I want Christians who were known by their afflictions to begin to praise the name of the Lord, speak words to your future. God is waiting for you to forget about what had happened in the past. Before God, you are not too late--it is early, and you are starting a new journey.

Where are your scars? Some of you have children who have different fathers; this is a scar. All of them resemble their fathers and the family keeps on mocking your Christianity, but very soon God will close their mouths.

Do not judge people by what they are facing. Let them talk when you are facing a permanent temptation; they know you cannot rise, but there's resurrection power that will make you rise and overtake. Some people even know what you always wear and eat, and others visit you to find out what is happening in your life--they have buried you, but they do not know that God is bringing you back to life.

They buried you knowing that you will not rise and become anything, but the angels of God shall descend to throw away the stone that was guarding you not to move. Those who were guarding you will never know how you came out. Jesus went out from the tomb and could go through where it was locked.

They have locked you up so that you may not enter, but you are entering, and they will not know how you entered. The question is-- what is it that has kept you there? Your friends seem to be succeeding; they seem to be living better than you, you have been buried and there was no way out, they left you because you were useless, but God is lifting you and you will be in front of them.

CHAPTER Ten

PRAYER

Luke 5:12-15

¹² And it happened when He was in a certain city, that behold, a man who was full of leprosy saw Jesus; and he fell on his face and implored Him, saying, "Lord, if You are willing, You can make me clean."

¹³ Then He put out His hand and touched him, saying, "I am willing; be cleansed." Immediately the leprosy left him. ¹⁴ And He charged him to tell no one, "But go and show yourself to the priest, and make an offering for your cleansing, as a testimony to them, just as Moses commanded."

¹⁵ However, the report went around concerning Him all the more; and great multitudes came together to hear, and to be healed by Him of their infirmities. ¹⁶ So He Himself often withdrew into the wilderness and prayed. (NKJV)

In the above scriptures, Jesus healed a man who was suffering from leprosy; there was no cure for this disease. Jesus only spoke a word, which created the healing.

Many times, when people were always gathering around Him, He could withdraw from them. Jesus never wanted fame, as He was supposed to canvas himself by the healing. Jesus walked away, and fame was searching for Him all the time.

Many Christians do not know the importance of prayer. Prayer is like gaining strength to work continually. Many Christians loose strength after being celebrated and fail to regain their strength.

The prayer you are making today is for your future. When you miss prayer today, you will be affected tomorrow.

Do not wait for the situation to become worse before you start praying. Whatever you are facing now, you will overcome it by prayer. Jesus could not wait for a testimony, for it was not the first time He had done such a miracle.

Different types of Prayers

1. Repeated Prayer

Mark 14:38-40

[38] Watch and pray, lest you enter into temptation. The spirit indeed is willing, but the flesh is weak."

[39] Again He went away and prayed, and spoke the same words. [40] And when He returned, He found them asleep again, for their eyes were heavy; and they did not know what to answer Him. (NKJV)

In the time of temptations, pray until you overcome the temptation. Jesus prayed a repeated prayer when He was going to be crucified on the cross; He spoke one word until He was strengthened.

If you want to reach another level of victory, you need to spend more time in prayer; when you are tempted, you need to move from strong faith to victory faith.

Note that there is:

- **Common faith**
- **Growing faith**
- **Temptation faith**
- **Strong faith**
- **Victory faith**

The time of temptation tells you that you have not reached a level where you will pray and receive. You overcome temptations by seeing where you are going. Your prayer must be of thanks to God.

2. Prayer of Confession

James 5:16

Confess your trespasses* to one another, and pray for one another, that you may be healed. The effective, fervent prayer of a righteous man avails much. (NKJV)

Prayer of confession is a prayer of healing; when Jesus says that your sins are forgiven, it is as good as receiving your healing. When you are in pain, go to God and ask for forgiveness. Your pain is a prayer check when you are a Christian; pain is not there to kill you, but it is there for you to be prayerful.

3. Prayer of Faith

Matthew 6:6

But you, when you pray, go into your room, and when you have shut your door, pray to your Father who is in the secret place; and your Father who sees in secret will reward you openly. (NKJV)

The prayer of faith is a prayer that every believer needs. When you want something from God, enter into your closet--meaning do not talk about what you want; keep it between yourself and God. The problem that many Christians are facing is this: when things are tough, they tell everyone around.

The God who sees in secret knows the pain you are going through. The moment you say "**I have faith in me**," you are connected with Him. Do not talk about what you are facing, but believe that God is doing it for you. If you speak to people about your problems, you will be exposing yourself, and as a result, it brings doubt in you.

4. Prayer of Intercession

Mark 13:33

Take heed, watch and pray; for you do not know when the time is. (NKJV)

When you intercede you will be actually telling God that you do not know the time of change in your life, but you want to see where you are going--that is, you will be having hope of where you are going but not knowing when you will reach your destination. Those who always pray have hope; they believe in God.

5. Spiritual Warfare -- Fasting Prayer

Matthew 17:21

However, this kind does not go out except by prayer and fasting. (NKJV)

Spiritual warfare is a prayer of fighting things that you cannot see physically. A Christian who does not pray is overpowered by satan (a prayerless Christian is a powerless Christian).

When satan overpowers you, he interprets everything for you; when you overpower him, you will interpret all that he is doing in your life. Christians face many challenges, but as children of God, we need to be on top of him.

Situations must NOT control your emotions or affect your direction. You have the power to change and direct your situation. Prayer can change what the devil is doing in your life; whatever you bind here on earth is bound in heaven. God is connected with you through prayer.

Works of Prayer:

- **Prayer is there for you to change things in your life.**
- **Prayer is there also to humble you.**

When God humbles you, He makes you suitable for your miracle. People may define you to be less than who you are; you are suitable for where you are going--what are you praying for? You are called by God Almighty, and you are on top of satan.

Jesus said, "I saw satan fall like lightning from Heaven." Your enemies will fall and will never rise up again! This will happen when you pray.

There are different kinds of phases in prayer, and one of the phases is of breaking the wall where your prayer seems to be not reaching above. When you pray, everything must come from the Word of God. When you pray in your language, the Holy Spirit in you will take over--remember, satan can dictate your prayer.

Romans 10:14-17

How then shall they call on Him in whom they have not believed? And how shall they believe in Him of whom they have not heard? And how shall they hear without a preacher? [15] And how shall they preach unless they are sent? As it is written:

"How beautiful are the feet of those who preach the gospel of peace,* Who bring glad tidings of good things!"*

[16] But they have not all obeyed the gospel. For Isaiah says, "Lord, who has believed our report?" [17] So then faith comes by hearing, and hearing by the word of God. (NKJV)

You cannot call upon the Lord if you do not believe in Him. Christians who do not know the Word of God cannot pray.

Jeremiah 23:3

"But I will gather the remnant of My flock out of all countries where I have driven them, and bring them back to their folds; and they shall be fruitful and increase. (NKJV)

A Christian who does not pray is limited. Do not allow yourself to be limited, so that you may have great and mighty things in your life.

Remember the Bible says that Elijah was a man like us, but he called upon the Lord. Call upon the Lord and He will answer you.

Do not look at yourself and judge yourself by your situation, because in your tongue there is life and death. Your prayer counts when it does something to the kingdom of satan. God wants to prove your enemies wrong, so whatever you ask from Him, you shall receive it in Jesus' name.

CHAPTER Eleven

SEEING YOUR DESTINY

Luke 10:23

Then He turned to His disciples and said privately, "Blessed are the eyes which see the things you see; (NKJV)

We need to ask God to train us to see. Many of us desire to see our destiny; the Bible states that God must train our eyes. Jesus was with His disciples when He told them that blessed are the eyes that see His wonders. I was learning about the issue of seeing and I came to realize that God wants us to see our destiny, and when we see, many of us will change the way we pray.

Do you know why many prayers are of complaint? It is because we cannot see where we are going. If God allows you to see that in three months you will have a car, you will stop fasting for that car. If God opens your eyes to see, your prayer will always be of thanking Him.

We cannot fast just to say thank you Lord, because we cannot see what God is doing in our lives. God must teach us to see.

Jeremiah 1:11-12

Moreover the word of the Lord came to me, saying, "Jeremiah, what do you see?" And I said, "I see a branch of an almond tree." 12 Then the Lord said to me, "You have seen well, for I am ready to perform My word." (NKJV)

Jeremiah said that he was just a youth and he could not even say anything, for he was just a boy. He was not seeing right because he was affected by his being.

We are affected by our present situations--God wants to reveal who we are to the nations but, we must be in a position to see who we are; if you do not see well you will be affected in your decisions.

Jeremiah was bound to learn and God trained him to see well. Your being and past have affected the plan of God for your life. God was not interested in showing the tree to Jeremiah but that He could test if Jeremiah was in His plan of using him or not.

John 9:39

And Jesus said, "For judgment I have come into this world, that those who do not see may see, and that those who see may be made blind." (NKJV)

You will always fail when you see yourself as a failure. When you face calamities in your life and you concentrate on them, they will misdirect you. God wants to show you your future, so why are you complaining?

Joshua was afraid when he followed Moses, for he began to think that Moses was very much anointed, but God gave Joshua a command that wherever he set his foot, he would overcome. See where you are going, mind where you are going, and do not stay in one place.

Genesis 3:6-7

[6]So when the woman saw that the tree was good for food, that it was pleasant to the eyes, and a tree desirable to make one wise, she took of its fruit and ate. She also gave to her husband with her, and he ate.

[7]Then the eyes of both of them were opened, and they knew that they were naked; and they sewed fig leaves together and made themselves coverings. (NKJV)

In the above verses, what affected the man and the woman was their sight. When the devil spoke to them, they looked at the tree and they saw that it was good to be eaten; they forgot that God had

commanded them not to eat from the tree.

They went ahead and ate the fruit they were forbidden, and they went out of the plan of God. Many of the situations we have gone through were for the judgment of our eyes. Many married couples today fight because what brought them together was the issue of eyes--they saw by infatuation.

We must not make decisions based on our eyes, so ask God to help you to see. "**Don't look at your problem but at the solution I am bringing,**" says the Lord. The reason why you are afraid is because you are not seeing what God is bringing; see what God wants you to see. You might look like you are down, but you are not down--look where you belong, that is, look above; listen when God speaks and do not be affected by what you are seeing.

Rejoice when you know where you are going. What are you seeing? When someone says you will not succeed, the problem is with their eyes. You can say things such as "**I'm taking over! I'm not poor! I am not sick! I am rich and blessed!**" Look and see yourself as a millionaire. The problem is that you are looking at your financial situation and your debts, not realizing that already you are out of the situation.

Isaiah 60:4-5

"Lift up your eyes all around, and see:

They all gather together, they come to you; Your sons shall come from afar,

And your daughters shall be nursed at your side. [5] Then you shall see and become radiant,

And your heart shall swell with joy;

Because the abundance of the sea shall be turned to you,

The wealth of the Gentiles shall come to you. (NKJV)

This scripture is telling us that you are looking down at your problems. Lift up your eyes and see your success and prosperity. Do not look down; lift your eyes and see ahead. You have been facing down complaining that your situation is not changing.

Look at what God is bringing and not where you are. A person who looks down is a person searching for things which are not visible. Do not worry anymore or complain about your situation; see your destiny through the eyes of God.

CHAPTER Twelve

SUPPORTING THE GOSPEL

Luke 8:1-3

Now it came to pass, afterward, that He went through every city and village, preaching and bringing the glad tidings of the kingdom of God. And the twelve were with Him, ² and certain women who had been healed of evil spirits and infirmities — Mary called Magdalene, out of whom had come seven demons, ³ and Joanna the wife of Chuza, Herod's steward, and Susanna, and many others who provided for Him* from their substance. (NKJV)

I realized that truly the Gospel needs supporters, and during the time of Jesus we know that there was no technology,

and Jesus used to travel distances. He used His means of going out and reaching people and this was because of the people who recognized His vision of letting the Kingdom of God known.

It takes recognition to partake of what God is doing, because of these people in the second verse; the ministry of Jesus was supposed to be difficult, for He was not alone--He had twelve disciples.

There were many times where Jesus could not eat, but His disciples could eat. We are to reach a point where we do not see the things of this world as important, but we need to reach out to the world.

For churches to reach out, we need these kinds of people who support the Gospel, making sure they are there and taking care that the Gospel is moving. Many people do not support the Gospel for a long time; many of the supporters of Jesus Christ were with Him until he was crucified. If this happened during the time of Jesus, it will happen during our time.

We need people who support the Gospel out of their substances. Take what you have and give it to God, and you will receive a multiplication; it comes by recognizing--meaning that you are aware, and making you to find a revelation that will bring results upon your life.

Mark 16:15-20

[15] And He said to them, "Go into all the world and preach the gospel to every creature. [16] He who believes and is baptized will be saved; but he who does not believe will be condemned. [17] And these signs will follow those who believe: In My name they will cast out demons; they will speak with new tongues; [18] they will take up serpents; and if they drink anything deadly, it will by no means hurt them; they will lay hands on the sick, and they will recover."

Christ Ascends to God's Right Hand

[19] So then, after the Lord had spoken to them, He was received up into heaven, and sat down at the right hand of God. [20] And they went out and preached everywhere, the Lord working with them and confirming the word through the accompanying signs. Amen. (NKJV)

Jesus here commanded His disciples to go and preach the Gospel (out of their means). This is a challenge to us, for we cannot do it without technology such as television and many other mediums which can be used to carry out the Gospel to the world. To be honest with you, I found out that many people on earth are sick--99.9% of them--and they need pastors.

No one can say that they are not facing challenges, for it is a challenge that brings sickness. The Gospel can be blocked if we do not have people who can say "**GO**." We cannot go to heaven if we are failing to see beyond.

Jesus in verse 20 never said goodbye. He was taken to heaven and the question that the disciples asked was "**Where do we start?**" Jesus just gave them the commission; therefore automatically they had to do things like Jesus.

1 Corinthians 9:11-19

[11] If we have sown spiritual things for you, is it a great thing if we reap your material things? [12] If others are partakers of this right over you, are we not even more?

Nevertheless we have not used this right, but endure all things lest we hinder the gospel of Christ. [13] Do you not know that those who minister the holy things eat of the things of the temple, and those who serve at the altar partake of the offerings of the altar? [14] Even so the Lord has commanded that those who preach the gospel should live from the gospel.

[15]But I have used none of these things, nor have I written these things that it should be done so to me; for it would be better for me to die than that anyone should make my boasting void. [16] For if I preach the gospel, I have nothing to boast of, for necessity is laid upon me; yes, woe is me if I do not preach the gospel!

[17] For if I do this willingly, I have a reward; but if against my will, I have been entrusted with a stewardship. [18] What is my reward then? That when I preach the gospel, I may present the gospel of Christ without charge, that I may not abuse my authority in the gospel.

Serving All Men

[19] For though I am free from all men, I have made myself a servant to all, that I might win the more. (NKJV)

We must reach a point whereby we come to realize that supporting a pastor is not a matter of doing the pastor a favor, but supporting the Gospel. Paul was saying that people need to support their pastors and that pastors must preach--not because they want anything from their congregation, but voluntarily by the will of God.

Philippians 4:14

¹⁴ Nevertheless you have done well that you shared in my distress. (NKJV)

Paul was saying that a pastor's preaching is spiritual because they give the Word, and you are to give back in material; that is, you bless the pastor materially. Your support touches your pastor, and it also touches the heart of God. It is out of the Gospel that someone recognizes the need to support a pastor, and out of the prayers of the pastor you are supporting, your prayers will be heard by God.

Heathens seem to be stronger than Christians, because Christians do not know the principles of going up. Know that as you support your pastors, God will supply you and your life will escalate. I am promising you that as you continue supporting your pastors, God will supply you.

CHAPTER **Thirteen**

TEMPTATIONS

Temptation is a step that you need to go through before you have a blessing. When you endure the temptation, you are blessed. Sometimes challenges come like temptations.

There are two kinds of temptation:

- **Temporary Temptation**
- **Permanent Temptation**

We face different temptations in life because of our destinies. As a child of God, one must be tempted. A heathen cannot be tempted, for whatever comes to him on the way is seen as an opportunity.

Temporary temptations are there just to delay us for the best--they are there simply to delay us. That is, any delay you face, God uses it to preserve you, because if you receive a blessing at a wrong time it will kill you. You are reserved for a purpose; you were out and saw other people overtaking you, but God knew what He was doing.

On Temporary temptation, God just puts you aside and when they run, He takes you from the side and puts you at the end and when they reach the end they will find you already there.

There is a temptation which is permanent, and which cannot be changed. If someone else were to use your surname, that rendered him/her weak and defeated, but as you are using the same surname, which is permanent, with that same surname God will prove your enemies wrong. When facing permanent temptation, know that the glory that will discern will make you a leader; it leaves a scar.

James 1:12-14
¹² Blessed is the man who endures temptation; for when he has been approved, he will receive the crown of life which the Lord has promised to those who love Him. ¹³ Let no one say when he is tempted, "I am tempted by God"; for God cannot be tempted by evil, nor does He Himself tempt anyone. ¹⁴ But each one is tempted when he is drawn away by his own desires and enticed. *(NKJV)*

Your temptation is working for your patience; all temptations that you are facing should be counted all joy. The moment you are a pastor, you will face temptations that pastors face.

I found out that whoever is preaching the Gospel must pay a price to reach a certain level. You are tempted because there are temptations and it is God who says enough is enough, endure and you shall be approved because you are fit for that temptation.

Whatever you face might be a temptation, but God does not bring these temptations, for satan is the tempter. Temptations come before the blessing; the Bible says "**Blessed are those who endure**," meaning you endure until you reach a point where God says you are fit.

If you get a blessing without enduring, the blessing can be a curse to your life. As long as you are living, you will have certain desires; therefore you will be tempted. Only those in the grave cannot be tempted. The work of a temptation is to check if truly you are a Christian--are you what you say you are? You are to endure in your failures and hold on to Jesus. I am telling you that as long as you endure, your day of victory will come.

Hebrews 5:8
⁸ though He was a Son, yet He learned obedience by the things which He suffered. (NKJV)

Temptations provoke your obedience; though Jesus was a son, He learned obedience by suffering. He endured the pain because of the joy that was set before Him, for He understood where he was going. We must know the end of our trials.

When you read about how Abraham left his family, you will realize that he left without God showing him where his destiny would end. We need Christians who cannot complain, who know the end before the beginning. When you hear pain and hunger, God might be saying that you must wait for a while.

Just like Saul from the book of Samuel, God will change your heart, and all things shall come to pass. When you are suffering from pain, God is speaking and saying that you should carry on. Jesus suffered and learned obedience from suffering; He did something that many of us cannot do.

In the book of John chapter four, Jesus was hungry as He was at the well; the disciples saw the need to go buy food, but He knew that He was there for His purpose in life and not to eat or drink.

When God takes you to a well, many of you forget the purpose that God has given you. Jesus was at the well not to drink but to change someone's life.

When you seem to be nearer to your well, do not think that you have arrived, for a well is not an ocean.

Move and go to your destiny. All the temptations you are facing are there to take you to a higher position. The moment you feel pain, you will worry about death but be different—instead, in the midst of your pain, get up and thank God. When you have lack and you are waiting for finances, just close the door and worship your God.

CHAPTER Fourteen

TO BE BORN AGAIN

John 3:3-4

³ Jesus answered and said to him, "Most assuredly, I say to you, unless one is born again, he cannot see the kingdom of God."

⁴ Nicodemus said to Him, "How can a man be born when he is old? Can he enter a second time into his mother's womb and be born?" (NKJV)

Many people say they are born again, but they do not really know that to be born again is more than a transformation. Nicodemus went to Jesus and said to Him that they (Nicodemus and other Pharisees) knew that He could not do the things He did if He were not from God. Nicodemus was implying that they were not coming from God and were leaders without power.

Jesus addressed Nicodemus on how he could get that power for himself, if he understood that Jesus came from God. For him to reach the level of Jesus, he must be born again. What Jesus was saying was very dangerous.Nicodemus' understanding was not at the same level as Jesus' level of understanding. Jesus was talking about being born again in spirit, and Nicodemus was talking about being born once (by the will of the flesh).

Jesus was saying if truly you need to be born again, you are supposed to live another life than the one you know. You must experience new things than those you have experienced. Nicodemus was already seventy years old and wondered how he could go back to being small and taught again to grow.

1 Peter 1:21-23

²¹ who through Him believe in God, who raised Him from the dead and gave Him glory, so that your faith and hope are in God.

The Enduring Word

²² Since you have purified your souls in obeying the truth through the Spirit* in sincere love of the brethren, love one another fervently with a pure heart, ²³ having been born again, not of corruptible seed but incorruptible, through the word of God which lives and abides forever. (NKJV)

If you are born again, you will be aware; you will have a revelation which will bring forth understanding. Listen, many people are going to church, but they lack awareness. Let awareness be revived, that you may be able to realize that what matters is not experience, but what God says. All your experiences and failures will not count or matter before God. If you are aware, you will see, and you will discover.

Unless you are aware, you will never find what will cause you to discover. For many of you, the reason you say you are born again and yet you are still sinning is because you have not yet discovered your life. When you are born again, you will realize and know that the life you were living before was not good, and you will not go to it again.

John 8:32

And you shall know the truth, and the truth shall make you free. (NKJV)

You will know the truth and you will be free; for you to be born again is to be living in freedom, and the life of the past should not matter anymore. Many of us do not know that to be born again is to be transferred from darkness to the Kingdom of Light.

In darkness you are not visible and you cannot see where you are going, but in the light, you know where you are going; you can discover and understand your destiny.

Ephesians 3:19-20

[19] to know the love of Christ which passes knowledge; that you may be filled with all the fullness of God.

[20] Now to Him who is able to do exceedingly abundantly above all that we ask or think, according to the power that works in us, [21] to Him be glory in the church by Christ Jesus to all generations, forever and ever. Amen. (NKJV)

When you are born again, you know where you are going; you have plans, but you are able to crush them and make new plans. You reach a level of knowing the love of Christ and by so doing, you will ask God, and He will do the same above. The reason we are not fruitful is because we undermine the stage of being born again.

The moment you are born again, you have sight to discover, to know, and you will be filled with the fullness of God; whatever you think about God will do it. If you are born again, realization comes; you can see and discover and know there are things that, when you mention the name of Jesus, will happen. If you are born of God, you are one with God; you will think like God, and what you think will happen. Do not lack the benefits of being born again. You were born into a family of lack; now that you are born of God, you can prove that all things are possible.

Romans 6:6-10

[6] knowing this that our old man was crucified with Him, that the body of sin might be done away with, that we should no longer be slaves of sin. [7] For he who has died has been freed from sin. [8] Now if we died with Christ, we believe that we shall also live with Him, [9] knowing that Christ, having been raised from the dead, dies no more. Death no longer has dominion over Him. [10] For the death that He died, He died to sin once for all; but the life that He lives, He lives to God. *(NKJV)*

TO BE BORN AGAIN

Check yourself--if your old nature is still there, question if truly you are born again. If you worry like a heathen, your birth in God is questionable. To be born again is to have the ability of the One who gave birth to you. The One who gave birth to you will never fail; therefore your nature will not allow you to fail.

To be born again, your character and your prayer life must change. Judge yourself and do not wait for anyone to judge you; look at yourself before someone else accuses you. The moment you understand that, when you think of something, it will happen and whatever you ask will be granted. The moment I knew I was born again, I said, "I do not want to be like anyone else, but like Jesus."

Revelation 1:6

And has made us kings* and priests to His God and Father, to Him be glory and dominion forever and ever. Amen. (NKJV)

You are not limited; you are like Jesus. You may be a failure, but it was of the past and as you are now born again, you are not in the place of distress. We need Christians who know where they are going and are no longer compromising.

We need Christians who are up and not down. You cannot waste time in prayer; before you pray, check yourself. Many justify themselves before checking themselves, and this is a mistake many Christians are committing.

Job 19:25-26

For I know that my Redeemer lives, And He shall stand at last on the earth;

And after my skin is destroyed, this I know,

That in my flesh I shall see God. (NKJV)

Job said though he had sores and it looked as if it was better for him to die, after everything that had happened he could still see God. A person who is born again is there to break records. Everyone born outside Jerusalem was regarded as nothing, because they had nothing to prove that God was on their side.

When Peter and the other disciples said that the Messiah was from outside Jerusalem, many did not believe in them. There are some people who know what is happening in your life but do not know your destiny. When you are born of God, when you come from a place that is not known, you will be a surprise to those who have rendered you useless.

I know that this God we serve does not care where you were born; He checks if He is the one who gave birth to you, and if He is the one, there is no sickness which will stay longer in your body. If you are born in a family of diabetes, you will come with a different blood status--your family can be poor, but you cannot be poor, for you know the one who gave birth to you.

You are different. We need Christians who know that they are born again. Many people may still be holding on to your failures and your wrong decisions; they mock your Christianity, but they do not know that God is able. Know yourself and do not wait for signs. Be that sign; God will make sure that you will not fail.

1 Corinthians 2:12

Now we have received, not the spirit of the world, but the Spirit who is from God, that we might know the things that have been freely given to us by God. (NKJV)

This Spirit that you are given when you are born again makes you to know. You pray direct prayers and not many idle prayers; there are things that you need to know that you have been given freely, and you do not have to pray for them. You need to be rich and healed, for that is free. By His stripes you are healed; therefore, you do not have to pray for healing.

There is a Spirit that will make you know that you are to receive things freely; for you to receive blessings, it is something you are to know and agree with. If you have received the Spirit of God when you are born again, which kind of spirit then makes you pray unnecessary prayers?

Romans 8:32

He who did not spare His own Son, but delivered Him up for us all, how shall He not with Him also freely give all things. *(NKJV)*

If God gave you Jesus without you fasting, then why do you fast for all that God has given you through Jesus? Your Father is very rich; you cannot be poor. When you are lacking to get what you want, it might be questionable regarding the kind of Spirit you have received.

If truly you are born of God, that poverty is a testimony--are you worried? You cannot compete with your enemies because you are not their type.

You are not that type of suffering, of shame, of falling, of lack, of unemployment; whatever you touch will prosper. Jesus is on your side; you cannot fail. You are succeeding in Jesus' name.

CHAPTER Fifteen

UNCOMMON CHALLENGES

LUKE 6:22-23

²² Blessed are you when men hate you, and when they exclude you, and revile you, and cast out your name as evil, for the Son of Man's sake.

²³ Rejoice in that day and leap for joy! For indeed your reward is great in heaven, for in like manner their fathers did to the prophets. (NKJV)

Many Christians like to devote themselves to fasting and prayer because of various situations they are facing. Christians are not there to be celebrated but are there to be tested, so that from those tests they may be able to get a testimony.

In many instances when things seem not to go our way, we start to lose focus and start to question if really God is with us or not. The answer is yes, for God is always with us in times of testing.

God sometimes allows it so that we can draw closer to Him to learn from His feet, but most of us see that as a punishment. For a true believer, challenges are good, as they are there to humble you or to refine you for extraordinary services. satan is actually keeping Christians busy so that they may not see what God is doing in their lives; God wants us to come in His presence in hard times so that we may learn at His feet.

There are many things happening around us, covering our miracles so that we may not be able to see what God is doing in our lives.

What you are facing is there to refine you to a better level. I thank God for your life today, because whatever uncommon challenge you are facing is there to call uncommon results from God. All the challenges you are facing are there to build you, for you are made up of challenges. Many challenges are there to establish you and build up your faith.

Many rejoice when they find themselves in this kind of situation, because they know that situations are there to take them to another step of crossing to the other side. I want to rejoice with you because the uncommon challenges you are facing will turn into uncommon miracles. The uncommon challenges you are facing are there to hinder you from seeing what God is about to do in your life.

Ephesians 6:11-12

Put on the whole armor of God, that you may be able to stand against the wiles of the devil. [12] For we do not wrestle against flesh and blood, but against principalities, against powers, against the rulers of the darkness of this age, against spiritual hosts of wickedness in the heavenly places. (NKJV)

The above scriptures are teaching us not to fight flesh and blood, because Jesus never looked at what they were doing to Him when they were crucifying Him, for He knew who was behind it. There are some people who, when they look at their situation, all they see is satan rather than God; they always talk about their problems, and that is why satan makes them lose focus.

God knows what you are facing, and He wants you to learn and get results from your hardships. The Bible instructs us to put on the full armor of God so that we may be able to withstand whatsoever satan will try to inflict upon our lives.

When you are wearing the full armor of God, satan will be there to challenge you, but you will win the battle. Many of you are being fought by agents of satan not to withstand; you failed to comprehend, for you could not tolerate, and you fell down, but I am here to tell you to rise up again--why? Because you can do it; this is your time.

Stand your ground. We need Christians who can stand their ground no matter the circumstance. Jesus is Lord; let your ground be established by God.

I have learned that every challenge we face in life is there to draw us closer to God. What are you facing? Know that you are close to God. The bigger the challenge, the bigger the blessing, I have been told by our Father God that what you are facing, which is uncommon, is about to go back to your enemies.

Job 1:1

There was a man in the land of Uz, whose name was Job; and that man was blameless and upright, and one who feared God and shunned evil. (NKJV)

When you read this chapter you will find something shocking--Job was upright and blameless before God. Whatever God instructed Job to do, he would do it. Job would always make sure that there was no sin in his house. The Bible says that job was blameless before God, and everyone around him knew that he was serving God.

Listen, the devil found an opportunity to go and tempt Job. He lost everything but did not lose his life. Your life is a license of telling you that God can still do something about it. Job was not overruled by any situation, and that is why later on God changed his situation--because he stood his ground.

The challenges you are facing are telling you that you are in a right position with God; you cannot face challenges if you are not in right standing with God. It is only when you are challenged that you really know the people around you. You will find that the people you trusted may be the ones who are fighting against you.

They will come with ideas that will make you lose focus; when that happens, just know that you are in a right standing with God. You will see problems coming in many directions, but do not worry--just stand your ground. We need Christians who can stand their ground and who do not worry about what people are saying.

CHAPTER Sixteen

WEAKNESS

1 Corinthians 15:58
Therefore, my beloved brethren, be steadfast, immovable, always abounding in the work of the Lord, knowing that your labor is not in vain in the Lord. (NKJV)

When Paul was speaking to the Corinthians, the church was having many problems, and many questions were sent to him. After Paul had encouraged them, many things that happened were there to shake them. He told the Corinthians that

when you are committed, you are to stay in the word of God; you will be unmovable and steadfast.

There are many things coming to move you. They are there to change the direction of your prayers, that you may lose focus. There are many things that can make you miss heaven. Let your aim and vision always be in accordance with the Word of God.

When you read Genesis chapter 3, you will realize that Adam and Eve moved from where God wanted them to be. satan brings temptations in your life to move you from where you were placed by God. satan is there to render you weak wherever you are weak and to hold you there.

If you are not recognizing where you are weak, it might be that you are ignorant or defending yourself.

There are people who do not want their weaknesses to be exposed. If you live your life always in your comfort zone and you do not come out, you will feel like you have arrived, and you will miss your blessings. You might not be seen by people, but God sees whatever you are hiding.

If God wants to use His servants, He checks both their strengths and weaknesses. The one to be used mightily by God is the one who is not afraid of showing his/her weaknesses. Many are suffering because they hide their weaknesses. Christians must be realistic.

Job 1:8

Then the LORD said to satan, "Have you considered My servant Job, that there is none like him on the earth, a blameless and upright man, one who fears God and shuns evil?" (NKJV)

In the above scripture, you will realize how satan was complaining about God's protection over Job. He (satan) came to God and spoke about where Job was strong. Satan was saying to God that if He wanted to know a Christian, it is when the Christian is weak, because many people worship God when they are blessed.

When the blessings come to an end, many will curse God. satan went to God with the idea to make a deal with Job. Job's real faith was to be seen after he had lost all his possessions. satan is there to prove to God that through your weaknesses, you are not what you say you are. You can be weak financially and also weak in your marriage; do not worry, for your connection with God is within your heart and the grace of God will bring reality upon your life.

2 Corinthians 12:8-9

Concerning this thing I pleaded with the Lord three times that it might depart from me. [9] And He said to me, "My grace is sufficient for you, for My strength is made perfect in weakness." Therefore most gladly I will rather boast in my infirmities that the power of Christ may rest upon me.

Many of you have prayed and fasted, but have seen no change and you end up questioning why God does not answer your prayers. If you concentrate on your weaknesses, you can miss the grace that God is bringing upon your life.

It might be tough--do not focus on the situation, and look unto Him, the Author and Finisher of your faith. You might have prayed numerous times, but there is grace that is sufficient for you. The grace of God is about to come upon your life to bring a change.

Ephesians 1:8

which He made to abound toward us in all wisdom and prudence. (NKJV)

God knows everything about you; therefore your weakness does not matter. Do not dwell in your weaknesses. Many of us talk about our weaknesses. A friend can leave you, but God will never leave you.

God said He will be with you until the end. He knows all that you are facing; people might have rendered you useless, but God will never render you useless. They can capitalize on your weaknesses, but they do not know that as they are speaking about it, God is already finishing His works in your life.

Jonah 1:2-3

"Arise, go to Nineveh, that great city, and cry out against it; for their wickedness has come up before Me." ³ But Jonah arose to flee to Tarshish from the presence of the LORD. He went down to Joppa, and found a ship going to Tarshish; so he paid the fare, and went down into it, to go with them to Tarshish from the presence of the LORD. (NKJV)

Your weakness is revealed when God speaks. If God commands you to rise up and you fail, that means you are weak. If you judge me by my situation, you are wasting your time, for you do not know how much I hear God. When God told Jonah to rise up, he (Jonah) replied by saying that he could not go there for he hated those people; he was weak and failed to obey God.

Any weakness that is there proves to you that you have failed in your temptation. The reason you cannot go to another level is because you dwell in your weaknesses. Many people want to change their weakness, but through the very same weakness God is saying His grace has come to bring change. Your response after hearing God tells us that your weakness might be there or not.

Do not judge a Christian by what he is facing. I spent three years praying and seeing no change until God said my prayer was not in His Word. God said He was the one to add more people in the church and not my prayers. Many times we try to take the position of God by telling Him what to do. Live a holy life and allow God to do His part to bring changes in your life.

Matthew 26:33-35

33 Peter answered and said to Him, "Even if all are made to stumble because of You, I will never be made to stumble."

34 Jesus said to him, "Assuredly, I say to you that this night, before the rooster crows, you will deny Me three times."

35 Peter said to Him, "Even if I have to die with You, I will not deny You!" And so said all the disciples. (NKJV)

Peter was speaking with his mouth but not with his heart. Peter was in the flesh and not in the Spirit-- "**I can't leave you,**" as he confessed. Jesus told him that he was going to deny Him three times, and truly it happened.

Peter persisted that he would be ready to die also. You are tested by what you say. His weakness was tested.

During the interrogation of Jesus before His crucifixion, John was by His side, since he was His brother, but Peter was far away, sitting with people at the fire. John remembered he was with Peter and that he should be closer to Jesus. They sent a girl to fetch Peter, but Peter denied by saying that he did not know Jesus; he moved away and went far from the door.

Another came and told him he looked like Jesus and John, but yet again he denied and denied for the third time. This is the weakness of many Christians--they were close to Jesus but now they are far away from Him. Today when we cancel your weakness, you will come close to Jesus. When He speaks, you will hear him.

There is no situation that will control you. The problem you have been facing was there to take you away from Jesus but now it will take you closer to Jesus. When you are close, you will be like a representative of heaven.

Many people were very good at hearing God but now they cannot hear God and are now crying-- why? They are not careful of their weakness; their weakness was there that they could recognize it and overcome it to come nearer to God. That weakness in your family is cancelled.

There are many people who are already far from God because of their weakness, but there is restoration. What you have lost is coming back. Just like what happened to Job, all that was taken from you is coming back.

You are coming closer to take your marriage, your car, your healing, and all that you have been praying for. Take your blessing, your heart's desire. You cannot take something when you are far away.

The woman who was bleeding for many years did not care about the crowd but cared about being closer to Jesus. She wanted to touch the garment of Jesus Christ. When you are closer, it is easy to take what belongs to you. It is easy to take your blessings. Are you closer? Listen, there is no disease above the power of Jesus Christ, and when you are closer, you can be restored.

CHAPTER **Seventeen**

WILLINGNESS

John 6:38-39

[38] For I have come down from heaven, not to do My own will, but the will of Him who sent Me. [39] This is the will of the Father who sent Me, that of all He has given Me I should lose nothing, but should raise it up at the last day. (NKJV)

I found out that we have a challenge every day, which is to understand and do the will of God. It is out of your willingness that you are tested and it is seen if you are fit for a miracle or not. Your willingness provokes your stand before God. You cannot say you are a child of God by obedience only without willingness.

Obedience on its own does not take you far, but with willingness, you will go far. God sometimes wants us to obey things we do not want to do, and often that is where our willingness is checked. Willingness is a step from obedience to your miracle; before you receive your miracle, your willingness is checked whether you are suitable to receive it.

Hebrews 8:6

But now He has obtained a more excellent ministry, inasmuch as He is also Mediator of a better covenant, which was established on better promises. (NKJV)

Our willingness must be that we are not just coming to Jesus but that we are genuinely seeking Him. The Bible tells us about Jesus and that He was there for us with willingness. If truly you understand that willingness makes us lose all to gain much in heaven, then you will know that it is good to have a signature of Jesus Christ rather than that of people.

Jesus said that He did not come to do His own will, since many where doubting Him; He was saying that what they were seeing was His willingness after His obedience because of where He was coming from. You will do things and compromise if your willingness is not checked. The Bible says that when God loves you, He chastens you, and that must not change your willingness.

Willingness itself produces joy and peace which surpasses all understanding, meaning that even in your difficult situations, your joy and peace will not be understood by people.

Isaiah 1:19

If you are willing and obedient, you shall eat the good of the land. (NKJV)

If you are willing to do what God says--that is, enjoying doing what God says--you will eat the good of the land; therefore, willingness and obedience bring provision. Jonah failed because God sent him to his enemies and this caused his willingness and obedience to fail also. Willingness produces peace and must not only produce peace but also joy and happiness that will be available in tough situations.

Psalm 37:4

Delight yourself also in the LORD, and He shall give you the desires of your heart. (NKJV)

When you have willingness, you enjoy serving God, and what you are praying for will come to pass. It was not easy for Abraham; his willingness was also challenged. The family might have told him that there was no God who could honor him in his old age; Abraham's willingness overcame what he was hearing.

Between you and your progress of willingness there is a time interval--a time interval of temptations. If you are willing today, God will check to see if you are fit for all His promises. I thank God that you do not know where you are going, for He will direct you. As the Bible says: "**The steps of a good man are directed by the Lord.**"

God does not talk about where you are going but where you are currently situated and the steps that you ought to take. We need Christians who do not worry about where they are going but who are simply obeying God with willingness of heart. He always does above what we think or ask from Him; just rejoice for He is setting a table in the presence of your enemies.

Climbing a mountain is not easy--you sweat and meet obstacles, but when you are willing, you will climb with joy. The joy within you must make you overcome so that you may go to higher heights.

Galatians 5:7

You ran well. Who hindered you from obeying the truth? (NKJV)

You need to ask yourself--what is the hindrance that makes your race difficult? Obstacles are not there to block the road you are on, but to cover you; you are not visible in the race, and you are checked but not found. Paul was saying that you were supposed to be somewhere by now, but because of the hindrances in your life, you are still in one place.

There is a delay because of hindrances and obstacles in your life, but all those delays shall be destroyed in the name of Jesus! Do not be ignorant, but check and look out for hindrances when you are running a good race in life.

When Jesus was preaching about willingness, He said, "There were two children who were sent to do a certain task. The first son initially agreed to commence with the task but later failed to fulfill what he promised to do. The second son initially refused to commence with the task but later went to complete the task at hand."

Hindrances are there to give you a reason not to do what you are supposed to do. The second son saw the hindrances but decided to face them.

Many people only obey to do that which suits their understanding, but sometimes God requires your obedience in tough times beyond your understanding. Obey with joy, and do not worry about the hindrances and obstacles in your life.

The problem we are facing in the church today is that willingness no longer exists. Many people are seeking God, going to church because of the problems in their lives; they do not have the willingness to serve God, but the day God solves their problems, they disappear.

The longer the willingness is in you, the more the blessings will last. We need Christians who are willing to follow Jesus. When Jesus chose His disciples, He did not tell them where they would be going; all He wanted was their willingness.

Repent of all your disobedience and unwillingness and ask to be led by the Holy Spirit in all that you do. God be with you! If God is raising you, He does not check where you come from.

PRAYER OF SALVATION

Have you accepted the Lord Jesus Christ in to your heart? Are you born again? For you to live a victorious Christian life you need to be born again and surrender your life to the Lord Jesus Christ.

If your answer is 'NO" or you are not sure, pray this prayer of salvation with all your heart:

Lord Jesus, I come to you today. I am sinner; I cannot serve myself. Forgive me of all my sins. Wash me with your precious blood. Set me free from sin and satan to serve the Living God. I accept you into my heart as my Lord and Saviour today. I cancel every agreement that I have with satan or was made on my behalf with satan in Jesus. I am born again! Thank you, Lord Jesus for saving me! In Jesus' name, amen!!

If you have prayed this prayer of salvation, you are now saved. You are now a child of God.

This is the most important stage of how to live a victorious Christian life. **Life is a journey--enjoy the ride as a child of God with the Lord Jesus Christ. Amen!**

CPSIA information can be obtained
at www.ICGtesting.com
Printed in the USA
LVHW020359050619
620202LV00018B/767/P